Copyright © [2024] by [Janice McQueen]

All rights reserved.

No portion of this book may be reproduced, distributed or transmitted in any form without written permission from the publisher or author, except as permitted by U.S. copyright law.

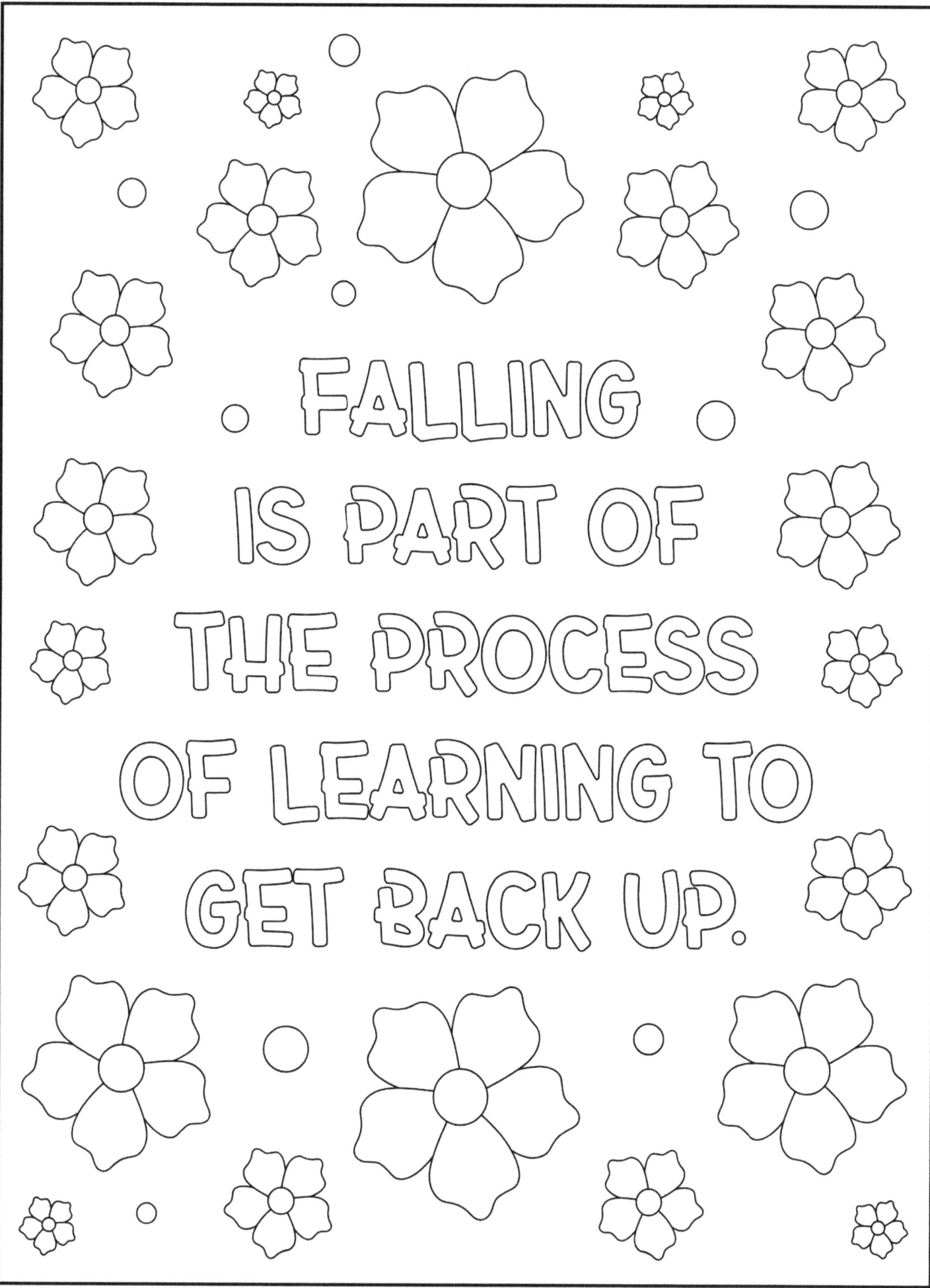

Share with your friends through feedback!

Help someone you've never met, even if you never got credit for it.
Who is this person you ask? They are like you. They Love Coloring Books. Share your enthusiasm and fun with coloring books by leaving a review to help people find the coloring books you enjoy!
Most people do, in fact, judge a book by its cover (and its reviews). So here's my ask on behalf of a struggling Coloring Book Enthusiasts you've never met:
Please help that Colorist by leaving this book a review.
Your gift costs no money and less than 60 seconds to make real, but can change a fellow Colorist's life forever. Your review could help...
...one more small businesses provide for their community.
...one more entrepreneur support their family.
...one more employee get meaningful work.
...one more Colorist transform their life.
...one more dream come true.
To get that 'feel good' feeling and help this person for real, all you have to do is...and it takes less than 60 seconds...

LEAVE A REVIEW

Thank you from the bottom of my heart.
- Your biggest fan, Janice.

www.ingramcontent.com/pod-product-compliance
Lightning Source LLC
Chambersburg PA
CBHW081324040426
42453CB00013B/2297